DATE DUE

DEMCO 38-297

Projects
That
Explore

Energy

PROJECTS THAT EXPLORE ENERGY

ENERGY

An Investigate! Book
by Martin J. Gutnik and
Natalie Browne-Gutnik

Illustrated by Sharon Lane Holm
The Millbrook Press
Brookfield, Connecticut

IN MEMORY OF
ITSY-BIT, PEANUT, RUNT, KITANAH, AND AMADEUS

Cover photograph courtesy of Photo Researchers

Photographs courtesy of NASA: p. 6; The Bettmann Archive: p. 13; Photo Researchers: pp. 28 (Ulrike Welsch); 58 (Alexander Lowry, 1990); U.S. Geological Survey: p. 50 (J.C. Ratte).

Library of Congress Cataloging-in-Publication Data
Gutnik, Martin J.
Projects that explore energy / by Martin J. Gutnik and Natalie Browne-Gutnik.
p. cm.
''An Investigate! book.''
Includes bibliographical references and index.
Summary: Presents scientific experiments that explore energy and its properties as well as the increasing problems of depletion of natural energy resources.
ISBN 1-56294-334-0 (lib. bdg.)
1. Force and energy—Juvenile literature. 2. Power (Mechanics) —Juvenile literature. 3. Power resources—Juvenile literature.
[1. Force and energy—Experiments. 2. Power (Mechanics)— Experiments. 3. Power resources—Experiments. 4. Experiments.]
I. Browne-Gutnik, Natalie. II. Title.
QC73.4.G88   1994
333.79—dc20   93-7787   CIP   AC

Published by The Millbrook Press
2 Old New Milford Road, Brookfield, Connecticut 06804

Contents

166415

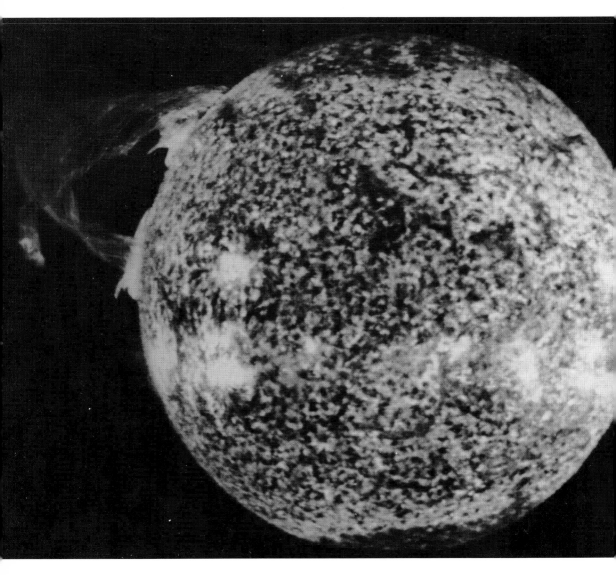

The sun, shown here, is Earth's primary supplier of energy. In the upper left is a solar flare, an eruption of heat and light energy.

1

Introduction

According to the *Big Bang Theory,* ages ago our universe was born out of a massive explosion. This explosion sent gases expanding outward. As they expanded, the gases cooled and particles appeared. These particles became matter. Matter collected into galaxies and then formed stars.

Our sun is one such star, formed billions of years after the explosion called the Big Bang. Around the sun smaller masses of matter formed planets, creating our solar system. One of these planets became Earth.

The explosion that created the universe, according to the Big Bang Theory, was a release of energy. Billions of years later that same energy is still powering the universe. It powers our sun, which provides the energy that makes life on Earth possible.

ENERGY AND LIFE

Life, as we know it, would not exist without energy. Solar energy on Earth creates the wind, the rain, and flowing water. It provides the fuel for *photosynthesis,* the process by which green plants make food for themselves and all other living things.

From the earliest stages of human history, energy and its use have been key factors in the development of civilizations and their ways of life. Early societies had minimal energy needs. People required food to live and fire for warmth, cooking, light, and protection from wild beasts.

As human societies developed, their energy needs increased. To meet these needs, people learned how to domesticate plants and animals. Animals were used as sources of power to plow and till fields. In addition, water was used to transport goods and wind was used to move ships.

People used energy in these ways for centuries—until the industrial revolution of the 1700s in Europe. The invention of the steam engine, and later of the internal-combustion engine, moved societies away from such forms of energy as water to *fossil fuels*—formed from the remains of plants and animals—such as coal, oil, and natural gas.

Fossil fuels have been the major source of energy for industrialized or developed countries through the twentieth century. As societies have become more industrialized, they have needed more fossil fuels for power. They have needed energy for massive transportation systems, to heat homes, and to light cities.

AN ENERGY CRISIS

Now, on the brink of the twenty-first century, societies everywhere find themselves in an "energy crisis." Fossil fuels are rapidly dwindling. Many say we have consumed our energy resources without giving enough thought to replenishing them or developing other sources of energy.

What is being done to deal with this energy crisis? In order to conserve energy and reduce fossil fuel consumption, many industrialized countries have developed *nuclear fission* energy. This involves obtaining energy by splitting atoms. Attempts have also been made to further develop solar power, wind power, battery power, and power through *nuclear fusion*, or the combining of atoms. These technologies are still in the early stages of development, however.

Some say that developing new technologies must go hand in hand with a massive energy conservation program and a better understanding of the energy dilemma.

EXPLORING ENERGY THROUGH
THE SCIENTIFIC METHOD

In this book, you will find out what energy is and how it works. You will explore the development of the energy crisis and what can be done to ensure energy supplies for future generations.

Before presenting projects that explore energy, it is important to point out that all science projects involve a method of scientific discovery. This method is known as the scientific method and includes the following steps.

Observation.   All science projects start with *observation*, using your senses to find out all you can about an object. In addition, observations can be made by researching a certain concept or idea and compiling the information you receive into a usable form.

Classification.   Compiling information is referred to as *classification*. This involves arranging objects or events in some order according to some property. A *property* is something about an object that helps to identify the object. Most objects have more than one property. So classifying is done to fit the classifier's needs.

Making an Inference.   Once information has been classified, the next step is to make an *inference* about the information. An inference is an educated guess, based upon what you have observed, about something that has happened.

Prediction.   A *prediction* is an inference about something that you believe is going to happen.

Formulating a Hypothesis.   The next step involves putting your inference or prediction into a testable statement. This statement is called a *hypothesis*. The hypothesis is the focus of the scientific investigation. All things done while performing the experiment must relate to the hypothesis. The hypothesis is usually in the form of an if-then statement.

Testing the Hypothesis. Once the hypothesis has been formulated, you are ready to perform the experiment that will test your theory. Your experiment MUST be controlled. Quite often there are *variables*, outside conditions that may affect the results of the experiment. Experimenters have to try to account for as many of these variables as they can, and that involves trying their experiments in more than one way. This is controlling the experiment. Sometimes, however, it is not possible to account for all the variables.

*Conclusion. After you have completed your scientific experiment, you must state whether your hypothesis was correct or not and why. This is drawing a *conclusion*. Conclusions can be stated in the following way:

> *Conclusion:* My hypothesis was (correct/incorrect) because (reason).

Often, an investigation will produce *results* that do not completely answer the questions you set out to answer. This means it is time for further investigation. When investigating further, the researcher must restate the hypothesis and investigate again. Don't be disappointed if your results are unexpected. Some of the world's greatest scientific discoveries were the results of experiments that went astray.

* Conclusions to all projects in this book can be found at the back under *Conclusions to Projects.*

2

What Is Energy?

Energy is the ability to do work. *Work* is the exerting of a force over a distance. A *force* is a push or pull on an object. Force creates motion.

NEWTON'S LAWS OF MOTION

Motion can be said to follow three laws formulated by the English physicist Sir Isaac Newton. In his *First Law of Motion*, Newton said that a body at rest will stay at rest until an outside force puts it into motion, and a body in motion will remain in motion until an outside force stops it. The principle behind this law is referred to as *inertia*.

Here is a good example of inertia. When you ride your bicycle, the outside force that creates the motion of your bike is the action of your feet on the pedals. If your bicycle is stopped suddenly by an outside force, such as a rock, your body will still move forward. There is no outside force stopping your body, which is moving at the same rate as the bicycle. If you slowly apply the brakes on your bike, your body slows at the same rate as the bike, and there is no inertia.

In his *Second Law of Motion*, Newton stated that a small force will move an object slowly, while a large force will move it rapidly. An object, moreover, always moves in the direction of the force. For example, a bullet moves quickly because the force behind it—exploding gunpowder—is large. The bullet also moves away from the weapon because the exploding gunpowder pushes it in that direction.

In his *Third Law of Motion,* Newton stated that for every action there is an equal and opposite reaction along the same straight line. A good example of this is bouncing a ball. After the ball hits whatever object it was thrown at, it bounces back, along the same line.

FORMS OF ENERGY

Energy can take many forms, and can be changed from one form to another. Some of the forms of energy are: light, heat, mechanical, and electrical. A windmill is an example of mechanical energy that produces electrical energy. The wind turns the blades of a windmill, which turn rotary engines or turbines to create electrical energy.

The Two Basic Types of Energy

In addition to various forms, energy can be divided into two basic types: *potential energy* and *kinetic energy.*

Potential energy is stored energy. Most objects, at rest, possess potential energy. A rock sitting on a cliff has potential energy. If the rock falls, that potential energy becomes kinetic energy.

Kinetic energy is the energy of motion. All moving objects possess kinetic energy. The more massive an object, the more kinetic energy it possesses. The faster it moves, the more kinetic energy it possesses.

LAWS OF ENERGY

As with movement, we apply natural or physical laws to energy. These laws help to explain why energy does what it does. Energy follows two laws, the first and second laws of thermodynamics.

An outbreak of the plague in the city of Cambridge forced Sir Isaac Newton, shown in this painting, to flee to the English countryside in the late 1600s. While living there alone, he began to realize his Laws of Motion.

The *First Law of Thermodynamics* states: Energy cannot be created or destroyed, but can be transferred or transformed. This law means that the amount of energy within the universe is constant. There will never really be any more or any less energy than already exists. As energy changes from one kind to another, or moves from one place to another, there is no gain or loss in the amount of energy involved.

Project #1—
The First Law of Thermodynamics

Background. As you know, there are many forms of energy, such as heat and light, among others. According to the first law of thermodynamics, energy can be and is transferred from one form to another.

Materials Needed

2 identical boxes about 30 x 30 x 30 cm (12 x 12 x 12 in)	plastic wrap
	scissors
2 identical tin cans (labels removed)	tape
	water
3–5 thermometers	measuring cup
dull black and white paints	graph paper
paint brushes	pencil

Observations. For this science project, your observations will come from what you see occurring during the activity and what you have read on thermodynamics.

Classification. The first law of thermodynamics is a scientific truth.

Inference. All energy can be transferred and transformed.

Hypothesis. If light is a form of energy, then it can be transferred and transformed.

Procedure.
1. Paint each box, one dull black and the other white. Let both dry.
2. Cut a window in one side of each box. Now tape a thermometer inside each box so that it can be read from the window. Cover the window with clear plastic wrap.
3. Place each box in a sunny place and observe the temperature in each box every ten minutes, for one hour.
4. Graph the results (see Figure 1).
5. Paint each tin can, one white and the other dull black. Let both dry.
6. Fill each can with an equal amount of cold water. Test the water in each can to make sure the starting temperatures are the same.
7. Take the cans and put them in a sunny spot. Put a thermometer in each can and observe the temperature in each can every ten minutes, for one hour.
8. Graph the results (see Figure 1).

Results.
1. Graph.
2. Light energy was converted to what kind of energy? How do you know this?
3. What happened in each box? Why did one box get hotter than the other?

Conclusion.   Was your hypothesis correct? Why or why not?

The *Second Law of Thermodynamics* states: When energy is transferred or transformed, some of it enters a state in which it becomes useless. This is a very important concept, especially when the energy source we are dealing with is finite, or limited.

Where does this energy go? Consider, for example, burning wood: When wood is burned, the carbon (C) in the wood combines with oxygen (O_2) in the air. Heat and light, products of the fire, are released and then lost in the atmosphere. They are not recoverable and are therefore useless.

Figure 1 - Thermodynamics-Charted Results

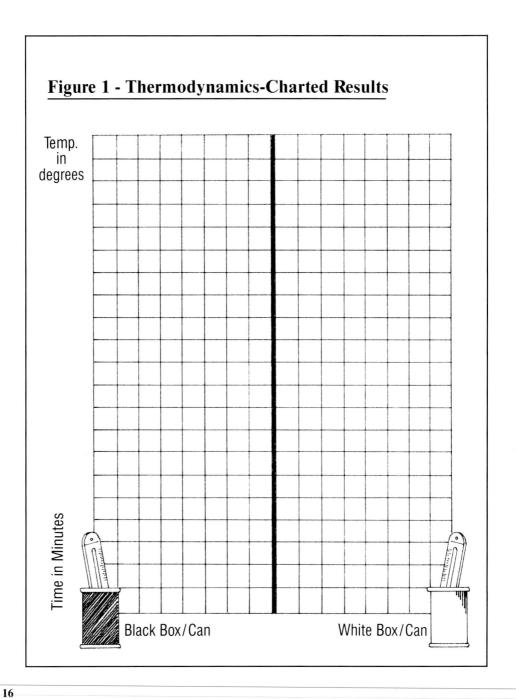

Temp.
in
degrees

Time in Minutes

Black Box/Can

White Box/Can

If some energy in transfer or transformation always becomes useless, won't we eventually run out of useful energy? This answer is yes, and in order to overcome this problem we must have a limitless source of energy. What is the limitless source of energy on Earth?

Project #2—
What Happened to the Energy?

Background. A *calorimeter* measures the amount of heat that will raise the temperature of one gram of water one degree Celsius. A calorimeter is used to measure heat gain or loss.

Materials Needed

electric hot plate

tongs

string

balance scale

13 x 13 cm (5 x 5 in) cardboard

10–12 metal washers

2 Styrofoam cups

a beaker filled with water

Celsius thermometer

compass

scissors

goggles

Observations. For this project, your observations will come from what you see in the experiment and what you have read about energy loss.

Inference. When energy is transferred, some of it becomes useless.

Hypothesis. If energy is transferred, then some of it will become useless.

Procedure.

1. Begin by making a simple calorimeter. Place one Styrofoam cup inside another. With cardboard, make a lid to fit inside the inner cup. Do this by measuring the diameter of the inner cup and then, with a compass, make a circle to that diameter on the cardboard. Cut the circle out of the cardboard. Find the center of the cardboard circle and punch a hole there, big enough for a Celsius thermometer.

2. Next find the weight of the calorimeter, by placing it on the scale. Record the weight in your results.

3. Fill the calorimeter one-half full of water and weigh it. Record this in your results. Subtract the weight of the calorimeter from the weight of the calorimeter one-half filled with water. Record this in your results.
4. Measure the temperature of the water inside the calorimeter. Record this as result #4.
5. Set a beaker filled with water on a hot plate. CAUTION: TAKE SAFETY PRECAUTIONS. THE PLATE CAN GET VERY HOT. USE GOGGLES TO PROTECT YOUR EYES. Bring the water to a boil. After the water has boiled, measure the temperature of the water. Record it.
6. Tie approximately ten washers together with a string. Make sure the string is long enough so that you do not have to touch the water. Place the washers in the boiling water. Boil them for several minutes.
7. Using your tongs, quickly remove the string of washers from the beaker and place them in the calorimeter. Observe the thermometer and record the highest temperature.
8. Examine your results. Was there a heat loss from the temperature of the boiling water to the washers? How many calories of heat were lost? Measure this by subtracting the temperature of the water in the calorimeter from the temperature of the boiling water. Was the mass of the calorimeter filled with water affected? How?

Results.
1. Mass of calorimeter empty.
2. Mass of calorimeter one-half filled with water.
3. Difference between result 1 and 2.
4. Temperature of water inside calorimeter.
5. Temperature of water in beaker.
6. Temperature of washers in calorimeter.
7. How many calories were lost?

Conclusion. Was your hypothesis correct or incorrect? Why or why not?

3

Ecology
and Energy

THE BIOSPHERE

On Earth, anywhere life can exist is known as the *biosphere*. There are only two places on our planet that are not part of the biosphere. One place is at the top of high mountains, where there is not enough oxygen to support life. The other is beneath Earth's crust, where both oxygen and light—also necessary for life—are absent.

Earth's biosphere consists of both living and nonliving things. Anything that was, is, or will be alive is considered a living thing. That means that a tree stump is considered as alive as an egg in the biosphere.

There are four nonliving things in the biosphere. These are air, water, soil (which includes sand, gravel, minerals, and rocks), and light. These nonliving things are necessary to support life. If any one of these is missing, life, as we know it, cannot exist.

ENERGY AND ECOLOGY

The science of how living things interrelate with each other and with the nonliving environment in the biosphere is known as *ecology*. Energy plays a key role in ecology. Within the biosphere, energy is absorbed by and transferred to living things through the *grazing food chain*. This term describes relationships between living things that depend upon one another for energy in the form of food.

All grazing food chains start with the process of photosynthesis. In the process, green plants convert *carbon dioxide* (CO_2) and water (H_2O), in the presence of light energy, into a simple sugar, glucose ($C_6H_{12}O_6$). The green plant absorbs light energy into its *chloroplasts,* small disc-like cells that contain *chlorophyll.* Chlorophyll is the only substance on Earth that can convert light energy into chemical energy. Once the chlorophyll absorbs the light energy, it converts that energy to *adenosine triphosphate (ATP),* a chemical. ATP is then used to split the water molecules brought into the plant. The water molecule is split into hydrogen and oxygen. The *oxygen* (O_2) is returned to the air. The remaining hydrogen combines with carbon dioxide to make *glucose* or sugar (see Diagram 1).

Green plants need water, carbon dioxide, and light to carry on photosynthesis. If any of these is missing, the process will not occur.

Project #3—
Photosynthesis

Background. Photosynthesis is the first step in the food chain. All the food on Earth comes from this process.

Materials Needed

4 geranium, impatiens, or coleus plants	water
	watering pitcher
bell jar, or a large mayonnaise or pickle jar	small plastic cup
	dark plant pot
soda lime crystals (a carbon dioxide absorbent)	masking tape
	pen

Observations. Your observations will come from what you witness during the procedure and have read about the food chain.

Inference. All green plants, in order to carry on the process of photosynthesis, need light, water, and carbon dioxide.

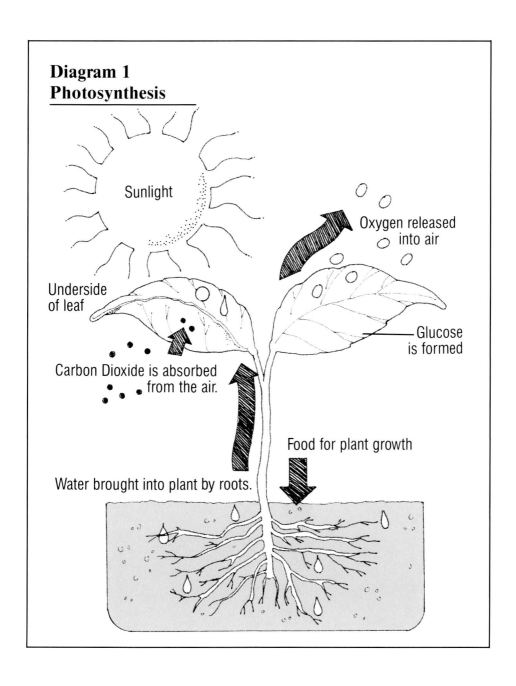

Diagram 1
Photosynthesis

Sunlight

Oxygen released
into air

Underside
of leaf

Glucose
is formed

Carbon Dioxide is absorbed
from the air.

Food for plant growth

Water brought into plant by roots.

Hypothesis. If green plants lack light, water, or carbon dioxide, then they will not be able to carry on the process of photosynthesis.

Procedure.

1. Take four geranium plants. With a piece of masking tape and a pen, label one plant "A." This will be your control plant. It will receive all the materials necessary for photosynthesis. Place it on a windowsill that receives plenty of light. Water it every other day. Watch it for one month. Once a week record its condition in the results chart (see Figure 3). If it is healthy, it is manufacturing glucose through the process of photosynthesis.

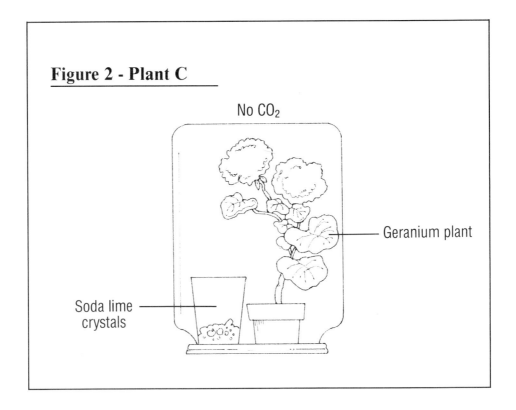

Figure 2 - Plant C

No CO$_2$

Geranium plant

Soda lime crystals

Figure 3 - Results for Project 3

	Plant A	No water Plant B	No CO$_2$ Plant C	No light Plant D
Week 1	Green and Healthy			
Week 2	Green and Healthy			
Week 3	Green and Healthy			
Week 4	Green and Healthy			

2. Label another plant "B—No Water." Take the plant and place it next to plant "A" on the windowsill. DO NOT WATER THIS PLANT. Observe the plant for a period of one month, recording its condition once a week in the results chart.
3. Label a third plant "C—No Carbon Dioxide." Obtain some *soda lime crystals* from your school's science teacher. Pour these crystals into a small plastic cup and place them next to plant "C" on the windowsill. Water plant "C" and cover it and the soda lime crystals with a bell jar (see Figure 2). Observe plant "C" over a period of one month and record its condition once a week in the results chart.
4. Label a fourth plant "D—No Light." Water it every other day. Cover it with a dark plant pot and keep it with the others. Observe it for one month, recording its condition once a week in the results chart.

Conclusion.   Was your hypothesis correct? Why or why not?

PRODUCERS, CONSUMERS, AND DECOMPOSERS

Since green plants are the only *organisms* (living things) on Earth that make their own food, they are referred to as *producers*. All other living things must exist on the energy transferred from green plants. These other organisms are called *consumers*.

There are several levels of consumers. Each level transfers food energy to the other. Organisms that receive energy directly from green plants are referred to as *herbivores*. Since herbivores are the first transfer of energy, they are called first-order consumers. Herbivores eat only green plants. Some examples of herbivores are: mice, bees, and rabbits. Herbivores store the energy from green plants in their flesh.

Carnivores are the next level up from herbivores. Carnivores eat only meat. There are two basic types of carnivores: carnivores that eat only herbivores (second-order consumers) and carnivores that eat both herbivores and other carnivores (third-order consumers). All carnivores are *predators* because they must capture their prey and eat it. Some examples of carnivores are: wolves, sharks, lions, eagles, and hyenas.

Omnivores, from the Latin word *omnis,* meaning all, are the next level up from carnivores. Omnivores receive energy by eating the flesh of animals, as well as by eating plants. Some examples of omnivores are: humans, bears, turtles, some birds, and raccoons.

Not all of the energy derived from food is used up by the plant or animal. Unused energy is released into the environment. When a plant or animal dies, moreover, it becomes stored energy that must be utilized. This waste and dead material become the fuel for the *detritus food chain.* In this food chain, organisms, such as bacteria, fungi, certain worms, and flies, eat the dead or decaying material and return it to the soil, in the form of *nutrients,* substances necessary for growth, to be used by green plants in the process of photosynthesis.

Project #4—
The Food Chain

Background. The background for this experiment comes from the material you read about the food chain.

Materials Needed
38–76 L (10–20 gal) fish tank and
   cover
11 kg (25 lb) of gravel
rocks
light for fish tank
aquatic plants (elodea)
2 snails (herbivores)
2 goldfish (omnivores)

2 crayfish (omnivores)
6 tadpoles (herbivores)
12 redworms or earthworms
   (omnivores)
aerator for fish tank
soapless steel-wool pads
pail
water

Observations. For this science project, many of your observations will come from what you have read about the food chain and what you see occurring during the procedure.

Inference.   Food chains can transfer the energy of the sun to living things.

Hypothesis.   If we create an aquatic food chain, then we will be able to observe transfers of energy to different levels of organisms.

Procedure.

1. Establish an aquatic environment by setting up a 38- to 76-liter (10- to 20-gallon) fish tank. This environment will represent a freshwater pond community. After obtaining a fish tank from your school or home, wash it thoroughly. DO NOT USE SOAP. Wash only with water and a soapless steel-wool pad.

2. Wash the gravel. Pour some of the gravel into a pail. Place the pail under a faucet and run water into the gravel until the water spills over the top of the pail. Reach into the gravel and stir it with your hands. The water spilling over the pail should now be cloudy. Keep stirring until the water spilled is clear again. This indicates that the gravel is clean.

3. Put the clean gravel into the bottom of the tank. Fill the tank one-third full of water and plant your elodea plants. Poke a hole in the gravel, and put the plant into the hole. Fill the hole (see Figure 4).

4. Once the plants have been set in, fill the tank to the top with water. Cover it with a lid and an aquarium light, which may be gotten from home, school, or pet store, and let the water stand for two full days. This will allow enough time for the chlorine to dissipate. The light should be left on for approximately 12 hours a day. This will give the plants enough energy to produce glucose.

5. After two days, add the other living organisms to the tank. Give these animals a day or so to establish themselves. Feed the fish worms every other day. Observe the tank each day for a month, and identify producers, herbivores, carnivores, omnivores, and decomposers.

Results.

1. Which animals eat the producers? Remember that green algae, one-celled plants that will grow on the glass of the tank, are producers.

2. Which animals eat the herbivores? The worms that supplement the fish's diet are herbivores.
3. Which animals eat the omnivores?
4. Were there any decomposers? What kinds? Perhaps an animal died in the tank. What happened to it?

Conclusion. Was your hypothesis correct? Why or why not?

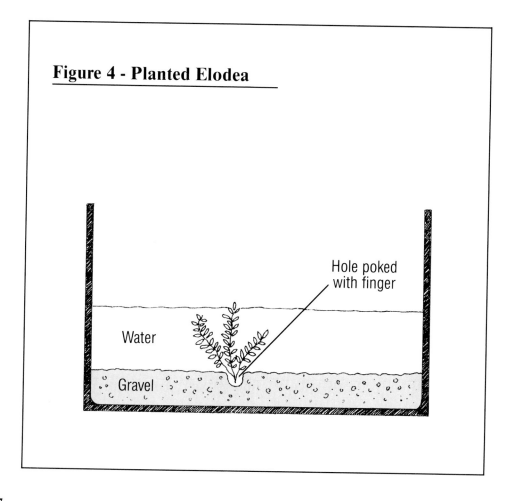

Figure 4 - Planted Elodea

Hole poked with finger

Water

Gravel

*From this tower, an oil drill bores into a Latin American
lake. The oil at the lake's bottom, formed millions of
years ago, will be brought to the surface and shipped to
a refinery. Then it will be used as a source of energy.*

4

Fossil Fuels

Many millions of years ago Earth's climate was much warmer, and the planet was covered, in many areas, with dense tropical forests. These forests consisted of large trees that grew in wet, bog-like soil. As these trees died and rotted, they fell to the ground and eventually became buried in that soil. The bog-like soil locked out the oxygen necessary for bacteria and fungi to decompose the trees. Because of this, the trees did not decay.

As the years passed, other layers of soil covered the trees and compressed them, turning them into *peat*. More soil covered the peat, compressing it further. As the peat became harder, from the compression, it formed coal.

The formation of oil and *natural gas* follows this pattern. The major difference is that these fuels were formed from microscopic plants and animals that lived in shallow seas. Many millions of years ago such seas covered much of Earth's surface. As these microscopic plants and animals died, they sank to the bottom and became buried in the muck. Just as there was not enough oxygen to decompose the buried trees, not enough oxygen existed to support decomposition. Over the years, the seas increased in size, and these tiny plants and animals were compressed under the layers of rock and soil. Eventually, they turned into oil and natural gas. Areas of oil and natural gas develop close to one another and are often discovered together.

Project #5—Coal

Background.   Coal can be found on every major continent in the world. It is still quite abundant, and its value lies in its ability to produce heat energy. However, much of the coal mined today has a very high sulfur content. When this coal is burned, sulfur fumes released into the atmosphere combine with oxygen to form *sulfur dioxide gas (SO_2)*.

Sulfur dioxide gas is a toxic substance that can cause lung and skin irritations in humans and other living things. When it collects with other gases in rain clouds and water from these clouds falls to Earth, it produces a toxin-filled form of rain called *acid rain*. Seventy percent of acid rain comes from sulfur dioxide gas.

Materials Needed

2 potted coleus plants (available at most garden centers)

2 bell jars, or large mayonnaise or pickle jars

wooden kitchen matches

water

2 aluminum pie plates

Observations.   All observations can be gotten by noting what happens during this project and from reading the previous pages on fossil fuels and the background to this experiment.

Inference.   Sulfur dioxide gas is harmful to living things.

Hypothesis.   If a coleus plant is exposed to too much sulfur dioxide gas, then it will be harmed.

Procedure.

1. Place each potted coleus plant on an aluminum pie plate and water it thoroughly. Allow a thin layer of water to rest in the plate. This will help to seal the jar when it is placed over the plant. Cover each plant with a jar. Label one jar ''A'' and the other jar ''B.''

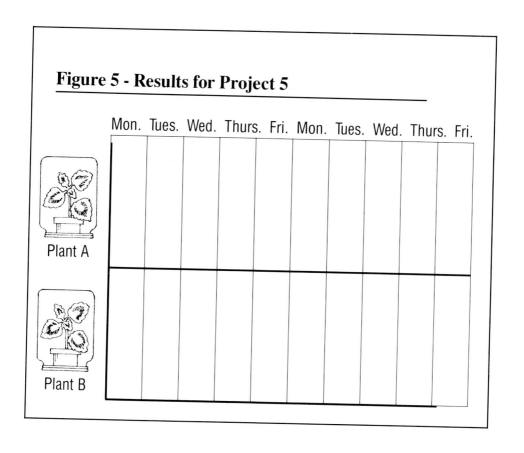

Figure 5 - Results for Project 5

	Mon.	Tues.	Wed.	Thurs.	Fri.	Mon.	Tues.	Wed.	Thurs.	Fri.
Plant A										
Plant B										

2. From Monday through Friday for the next two weeks, tip jar "A," allowing air to enter. Ten seconds should be sufficient. Tip Jar "B" just enough to fit your hand in the opening. Have your teacher or other adult light a kitchen match under jar "B," and hold it under the jar until it burns out. Do this once a day from Monday through Friday for two weeks.

3. Observe the plants each day and record the results (see Figure 5).

Conclusion. Was your hypothesis correct? Why or why not?

Project #6—Oil

Background. What about the effect of oil on living things? Oil, or *petroleum,* is the most widely used fossil fuel today, fulfilling 40 percent of all the energy needs in the United States. Petroleum is used to make gasoline and other fuels. It is also used in the manufacture of many other products that help to maintain our way of life.

Petroleum must be brought to the surface and carried to refineries. The shipment of oil has proven to be environmentally dangerous. Much of the world's oil is transported by ships or tankers. If one of these tankers gets into an accident, oil can leak into the water.

Oil is lighter than water and, when spilled, floats on the water's surface. Spilled oil blocks light from penetrating the water's surface, which prevents aquatic plants from carrying on photosynthesis. It also reduces the amount of oxygen in the water. All aquatic animals need *dissolved oxygen* in water to live. When aquatic animals, such as birds, seals, and otters, become covered with oil, they may suffocate or be poisoned. The oil also prevents their natural insulation from working, so that in colder areas many aquatic animals may die of exposure.

Materials Needed

2 fishbowls	2 healthy elodea (aquatic) plants
gravel	a measuring cup
water	motor oil (can be purchased at any gas
a pitcher	station)

Observations. Observations can be gotten by reading the material on fossil fuels and oil and by noting what happens during this project.

Inference. Oil spills can be harmful to aquatic environments.

Hypothesis. If oil is spilled on the surface of water, then it will prevent the aquatic plants from carrying on the process of photosynthesis.

Procedure.

1. Set up the fishbowls, following the same procedure as for setting up an aquatic environment in Project #4. Label one bowl "A" and the other bowl "B." Place both bowls close to a light source, preferably on a windowsill.

2. Pour one cup of oil onto the water's surface in bowl "A." For the next two weeks, observe the plants in each bowl and record the results from Monday through Friday.

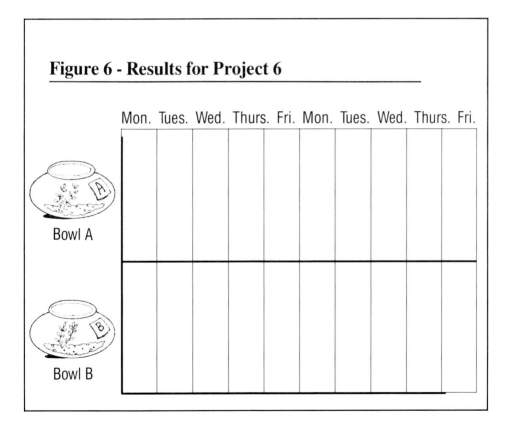

Figure 6 - Results for Project 6

	Mon.	Tues.	Wed.	Thurs.	Fri.	Mon.	Tues.	Wed.	Thurs.	Fri.
Bowl A										
Bowl B										

3. At the end of the two-week period, diagram the results of your project. Show the differences in the plants in each bowl (see Figure 6).

Conclusion. Was your hypothesis correct?

BURNING FOSSIL FUELS

When burned, fossil fuels cause more environmental damage than any other energy source. Most fossil fuels are burned in furnaces or in *internal-combustion engines.* This is an engine in which fuel is burned within the engine itself, rather than in an external furnace. One type of internal-combustion engine is the gasoline piston engine in a car.

Both external furnaces and internal-combustion engines do not burn fossil fuels completely, because they do not utilize enough oxygen. Oxygen is needed for objects to burn. Without a sufficient supply of oxygen, the fuels cannot burn completely. As a result, harmful gases and chemicals are emitted when fossil fuels are burned. These gases and chemicals—carbon dioxide, carbon monoxide, nitrous oxide, nitrogen dioxide, and sulfur dioxide—contribute to *ozone* depletion, and smog.

According to early 1990s estimates, fossil fuel combustion adds approximately 4.9 billion metric tons (5.5 billion tons) of carbon to the atmosphere each year. Much of this carbon is in the form of carbon dioxide gas. The combustion of coal and oil also adds tons of sulfur dioxide gas into the atmosphere. The combination of all these pollutants is damaging the natural systems within the biosphere.

Project #7—
Incomplete Combustion

Background. In addition to the poisonous gases and chemicals mentioned in the previous pages, *incomplete combustion* of fossil fuels causes the accumulation of carbon soot and *particulates.* Particulates are particles in the air. These polluting particles can get into the lungs and pores of living things and cause illness. Carbon soot is a particulate that specifically comes from incomplete combustion of fossil fuels.

Materials Needed

2 10 x 10 cm (4 x 4 in) tagboard cards   a magnifying glass
petroleum jelly (Vaseline)   any 2 automobiles

Observations.   Your observations will come from what you see happening during the procedure and what you have read about fossil fuels.

Inference.   Burning fossil fuels emits harmful chemicals, gases, and particulates into the atmosphere.

Hypothesis.   If fossil fuels are burned incompletely, then harmful particulates will be released into the atmosphere.

Procedure.

1. Prepare two white tagboard squares 10 x 10 centimeters (see Figure 7). Smear a fingerful of Vaseline in the center of the card. Ask your teacher or other adult to start his or her car, and MAKE CERTAIN IT IS IN THE PARK GEAR, AND THAT THE HAND BRAKE IS SET. Allow the car to run for about one minute.
2. Now hold your card about 2.5 centimeters (1 inch) from the end of the car's exhaust pipe. BE CAREFUL NOT TO BREATHE IN THE EXHAUST FUMES. TURN YOUR HEAD AWAY. ALSO, DO NOT TOUCH THE PIPE. IT MAY BE HOT. Make sure the Vaseline-covered area is in line with the exhaust opening. Hold the card in this position for about one minute.
3. Get the necessary information about the make and model of the car, number of cylinders, and date of last tune-up from the driver and write it down at the top of the card.
4. Repeat this same procedure on a second car. Examine each card with a magnifying glass. How are the cards different? What factors can

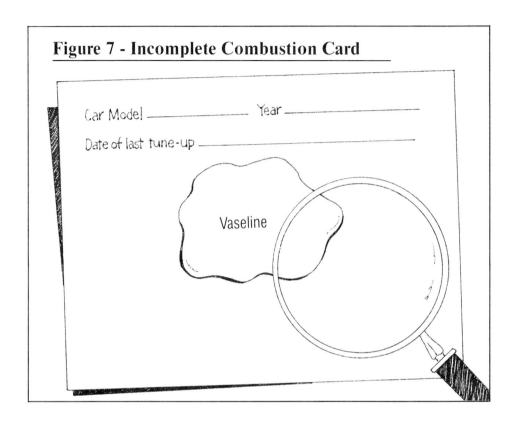

Figure 7 - Incomplete Combustion Card

Car Model _____ Year _____

Date of last tune-up _____

Vaseline

you think of to account for these differences? Variations in the ages of the car? Number of cylinders? How recently each had a tune-up? How can these particles you see be harmful? How do these experiments show the harmful effects of incomplete combustion? How does this type of burning waste energy?

Results.
1. What was on the card?
2. What happened to the card?

Conclusion. Was your hypothesis correct? Why or why not?

5

The Fossil Fuel Crisis and Alternative Forms of Energy

FOSSIL FUEL SHORTAGE

As we have seen, fossil fuels can be environmentally damaging. They are, moreover, in increasingly short supply. According to estimates made during the early 1990s, enough oil exists to meet the world's needs for approximately the next 50 to 75 years. A roughly 50-year supply of natural gas and a 200-year supply of coal remain. By almost any standard, the world shortage of fossil fuels has reached a crisis level.

FOSSIL FUELS AND DEVELOPMENT

The effects of this shortage have already become apparent. One effect has been the unequal development of nations throughout the world. During the twentieth century, developed nations, such as the United States, have grown into massive energy consumers. They have required more and more fossil fuels for the industries that power their economies and maintain the high standards of living that large numbers of their populations enjoy. Meanwhile, underdeveloped countries, such as Brazil, have struggled to develop technology and industries to improve their poor economies and raise their low living standards.

This has led to extreme inequalities between developed and underdeveloped countries. According to some people, these inequalities may never be leveled. By draining significant amounts of the world's dwindling energy supplies, people argue, developed countries have made it all but impossible for underdeveloped countries to catch up.

OIL AND POLITICS

As the world's energy supplies dwindle there is greater likelihood that nations will fight over them. The 1990–1991 war in the Persian Gulf took place, many believe, because the United States feared that Iraq would attempt to control oil supplies once it invaded its neighbor Kuwait.

ALTERNATIVE FORMS OF
ENERGY: SOLUTIONS?

What is to be done? Does our dependence on fossil fuels doom us to live in a world that is forever unfair? Will your generation find itself increasingly called upon to go to war to protect the world's oil supplies? Will our appetite for fossil fuels lead us to lay waste to our environment?

These are crucial questions. One answer is to use less fossil fuel energy. In addition to conservation—to be explored in Chapter 6—many suggest the development and use of alternative sources of energy.

During the early 1990s, renewable sources of energy accounted for approximately 10 percent of the domestic energy production of the United States. Initiating a policy for using clean, renewable energy sources at that time would meet 80 percent of the U.S. domestic energy needs by the early part of the 21st century. What might be the "clean, renewable energy sources" to accomplish this task?

Solar Energy

Sunlight, Earth's original source of energy, supplies as much energy in two days as all the remaining fossil fuel reserves in the world. How can this massive energy supply be put to use? A *solar-thermal energy system* collects the sun's energy and uses it to heat liquids. Commercially, this heated liquid then can be used to generate steam, which can be used to turn turbines for electrical power. The steam can also be used for heating purposes.

A well-designed solar-thermal heating system in a home can reduce the cost of heat energy by as much as 85 percent. During the early 1990s, approximately a million solar hot-water systems and 120,000 space-heating systems were operating in North America.

Other Forms of Solar Energy

Photovoltaic energy takes the energy of the sun and converts it directly into electricity. Light is converted into electricity when it hits a special type of solid-state cell composed of thin layers of semiconductor material. Some scientists are working on photovoltaic cells that use their electricity to split the molecule of water into its component parts of two hydrogen and one oxygen atoms. As the water splits, the hydrogen molecules are captured and processed as fuel for automobiles, homes, and industry. As the hydrogen is burned, it recombines with the oxygen in the atmosphere and creates more water.

Solar cooking uses focused light energy from the sun to cook food. A solar cooker is basically a solar collector. By focusing the sun's rays, it generates enough heat to cook food.

Project #8—
A Solar Cooker

Materials Needed

hot dogs	tape
cardboard boxes	an awl (for poking holes)
aluminum foil	posterboard (tagboard)
unpainted metal coat hanger	Fahrenheit meat thermometer
metric ruler	pencil and paper
rubber cement	scissors

Observations.   Your observations will come from what you note occurring during the activity and what you have read about solar energy.

Inference.   Sunlight can be used to cook food.

Hypothesis.   If sunlight is focused, then it can cook a hot dog.

Procedure.
1. Cut a tagboard sheet to 30 x 60 centimeters (11 × 22 inches). Curl
   the posterboard lengthwise, in a semicircular shape (see Figure 8).
2. Cut two pieces of cardboard 35 x 35 centimeters (13 × 13 inches).
   These will be the sides of your solar cooker. Use tape to attach the
   curled tagboard to the cardboard sides of the cooker (see Figure 9).

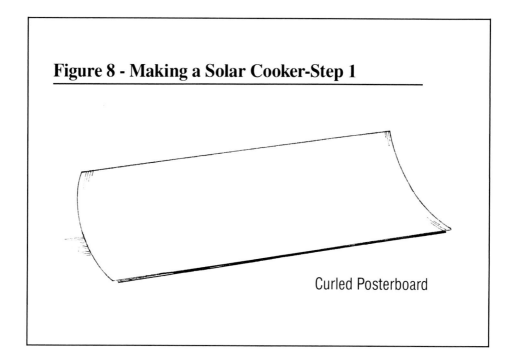

Figure 8 - Making a Solar Cooker-Step 1

Curled Posterboard

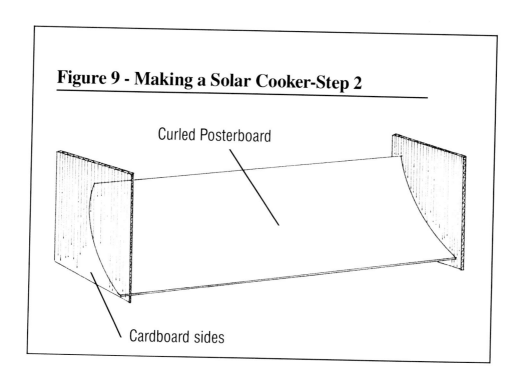

Figure 9 - Making a Solar Cooker-Step 2

Curled Posterboard

Cardboard sides

3. Cut three sheets of aluminum foil to the size of the curled tagboard and to fit the inside of each cardboard side of the cooker. Put the foil on these areas, shiny side out. Attach the foil to the tagboard and cardboard with rubber cement, on the dull surface of the foil. Carefully lay the foil over the tagboard and cardboard and smooth it down.

4. Straighten the coat hanger and bend one end into a handle. Use your awl to poke a hole in each cardboard side of the solar cooker. Measure to make sure the holes are at an equal height on each side.

5. Put the hanger through one side of the cooker. Skewer a hot dog. Put the hanger through the other side (see Figure 10).

6. Place your solar cooker in an area of bright sunlight, making sure the reflecting surface faces the sun. The sun's rays will strike the foil and cross on the focal points. A focal point is a point where the rays of

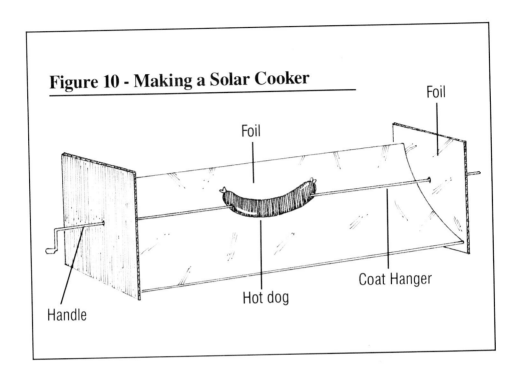

Figure 10 - Making a Solar Cooker

Foil

Foil

Hot dog

Coat Hanger

Handle

light come together and then spread out again. It is at the focal points where the heat from the sunlight is greatest.

7. Turn your hot dog while it is cooking, so that it cooks evenly. Time how long it takes your hot dog to cook. You will know the hot dog is done when the skin bubbles or splits. Record the time in your results. Use a thermometer to check the temperature inside the cooker when the hot dog is done. Record the temperature in your results.

Results.
1. How long did it take the hot dog to cook?
2. What was the cooker's temperature when the hot dog was done?

Conclusion.   Was your hypothesis correct? Why or why not?

Wind Power

The wind is solar energy in motion. On Earth, the sun's rays warm the air at the equator. This heated air rises, while colder air, from the polar regions, funnels in to replace it. This movement, plus the rotation of Earth, creates the wind.

The difference in the air's temperature creates the difference in weight in warm air and cold air. Warm air, such as air at the equator, is light and less dense. It is called low-pressure air. Cold air, such as at the poles, is heavier and more dense. It is called high-pressure air. On Earth, wind flows constantly from high pressure (cold air) to low pressure (warm air). This flow is known as the *pressure gradient force,* and it accounts for patterns in the wind's movement. In the Northern Hemisphere, wind moves counterclockwise into the center of a low-pressure system. Winds move clockwise out of high-pressure air.

The wind is a great potential renewable energy resource. Wind may be used to generate electrical and hydraulic power systems.

In the early 1990s, there were approximately 20,000 wind turbines (windmills) in the United States, generating the equivalent of 3.5 million barrels of oil annually. A key step in harnessing the wind's energy involves determining the wind's direction and speed.

Project #9—
Measuring the Wind
and Its Direction

Background. The background for this experiment comes from reading the previous section on wind.

Materials Needed—Part I

a block of wood, 20 x 20 x 4 cm (8 x 8 x 2 in)

2 balsa wood strips, 35 x 1 cm (14 x 0.4 in)

1 cm wood dowel

a pushpin

a stapler, with staples

modeling clay

plastic milk or juice carton	a compass
2 small metal washers	all-purpose glue
10-cm (4-in) diameter cardboard disc	an awl
	scissors
aluminum foil	ruler or yardstick
tape	pen or pencil

Materials Needed—Part II

Beaufort Scale for Measuring Wind in Knots

Beaufort #	Wind	Speed in Knots	Effects of Wind
0	calm	0–1	smoke rises straight up
1	light air	1–3	smoke drifts slowly
2	light breeze	4–6	leaves rustle, wind vane moves
3	gentle breeze	7–10	leaves/twigs move, flag is full
4	moderate breeze	11–16	small branches move
5	fresh breeze	17–21	small trees sway
6	strong breeze	22–27	large branches sway
7	moderate gale	28–33	whole trees bend
8	fresh gale	34–40	twigs break off trees
9	strong gale	41–47	branches break
10	whole gale	48–55	trees snap and blow down
11	storm	56–63	widespread damage occurs
12	hurricane	64–71	extreme damage occurs

Observations. For this science project, your observations will come from what you have read and experienced about wind and the Beaufort Scale.

Inference. In the Northern Hemisphere, winds blow counterclockwise (west to east) out of low-pressure systems.

Hypothesis. If a wind vane is constructed and used with a Beaufort Scale, then the direction and speed of the wind can be determined.

Procedure for Parts I and II.

1. Build a wind vane. Make your base from a block of wood 20 x 20 x 4 centimeters (8 x 8 x 2 inches). Place the wood on a working surface and find its center. At the center, place a drop of all-purpose glue. Take a dowel, 30 x 1 centimeters (11 x 0.4 inches), and put a drop of glue on one end and set it in the center of the wood base. Mold modeling clay around the area, to secure it (see Figure 11).

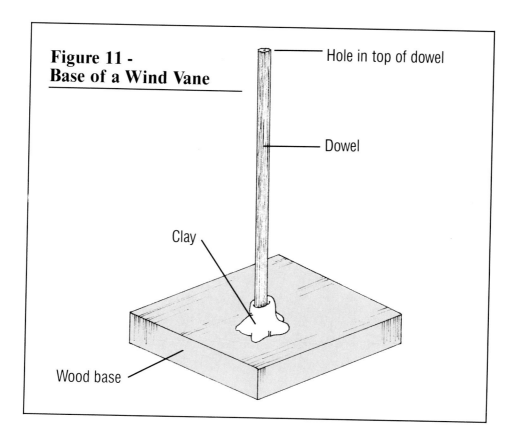

**Figure 11 -
Base of a Wind Vane**

Hole in top of dowel

Dowel

Clay

Wood base

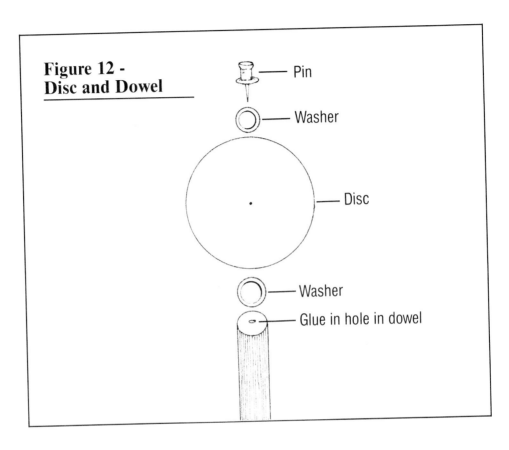

Figure 12 -
Disc and Dowel

Pin

Washer

Disc

Washer

Glue in hole in dowel

2. Allow the glue to set about 24 hours. Using the awl, punch a small hole in the center of your cardboard disc. Also punch a small hole in the top of your wood dowel (see Figure 12). Attach the disc to the dowel with a pushpin and two washers (see Figure 12). Put a small drop of glue in the hole in the dowel to secure the pushpin.

3. Cut two pieces of plastic from the milk carton, into 10 x 10 centimeter (4 x 4 inch) squares. Outline an arrowhead in one plastic square and a feather in the other (see Figure 13), and cut them out.

4. Glue each balsa wood strip, at its center, to the side of the disc. Use tape to secure the strips until the glue sets (see Figure 14).

Figure 13 - Arrowhead and Feather

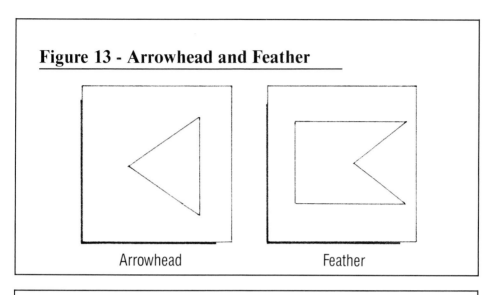

Arrowhead

Feather

Figure 14 - Balsa Strips Attached

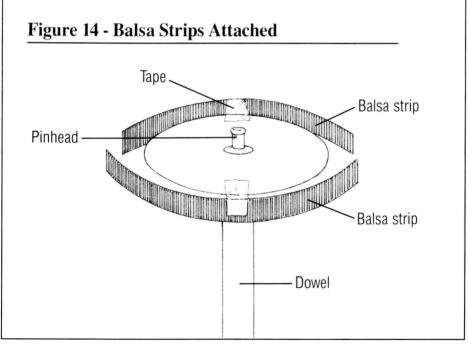

Tape

Balsa strip

Pinhead

Balsa strip

Dowel

5. Once the glue holding the strips is set, carefully bend one end of the strips together, inserting the plastic arrowhead between them. Press the strips to the center of the arrowhead and staple them in place. Follow the same procedure for the feather-like tail (see Figure 15).
6. Place your wind vane outside, in an area that is open. Observe the vane and how it responds to the wind. Use your compass to see which direction the wind is blowing. Record this in your results. Do this for a period of two weeks.
7. Use the Beaufort Scale to measure the velocity of the wind. Record this in your results.

Results. Make a chart to show wind direction and wind speed for a period of two weeks.

1. Based on your chart, how reliable was the wind direction during this two-week period?
2. Based on the Beaufort Scale, how varying was the force of the wind during this two-week period?
3. Based on your results for the wind's direction and force, how feasible is wind power as an energy source in your area?

Conclusion. Was your hypothesis correct? Why or why not?

Geothermal

Approximately forty miles beneath the surface of Earth lies a dense layer of gases and molten rock, called magma. This magma is created by great heat and pressure, from the surface of the earth and from the decay of radioactive substances beneath the surface. The temperature of the magma is approximately 1,650 degrees Celsius (3,000 degrees Fahrenheit).

Examples of this underground source of heat energy can be found in volcanic eruptions and the hot water expelled by geysers. Cracks in the surface layer of the earth allow the heat and pressure to rise and escape.

Figure 15 - Wind Vane

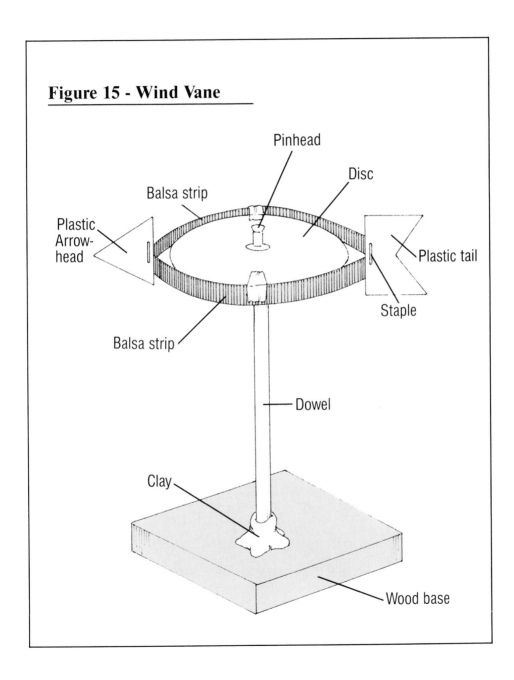

Pinhead

Disc

Balsa strip

Plastic
Arrow-
head

Plastic tail

Staple

Balsa strip

Dowel

Clay

Wood base

The volcanic eruption shown in this photo presents one type of geothermal energy. Other types are derived from geysers and from steam released from inside the earth.

If harnessed, the heat from these underground forces can be brought to the surface, in the form of steam and hot water. The steam, or hot water, can be used to turn the turbines of a generator, to produce electricity.

Already in use in California, New Zealand, Iceland, and Italy, *geothermal energy* is virtually limitless. For this reason, many believe that money should be made available to develop and improve geothermal systems. Geothermal energy could produce large amounts of electricity, without any significant damage to the environment.

Biomass

When a living thing dies or becomes waste, its energy-producing potential is far from over. Dead cornstalks can be converted into alcohol, which, when mixed with gas, can be made into gasohol, a fuel that can be used to run engines. Animal wastes, such as manure, can be burned for heat. This type of energy source is referred to as *biomass.*

Biomass is the oldest form of energy known to people. In farming societies, people have burned plant and animal material for heat energy and for cooking and lighting. Today, biomass is still the main source of energy for over half of Earth's population.

The advantages of biomass as a fuel are that it is readily accessible and renewable. The disadvantage is that, when burned, it adds carbon dioxide to the atmosphere. Carbon dioxide is a major gas that contributes to the *greenhouse effect.*

Many believe that this energy source should be used to supplement liquid and gas fuels. This will reduce the consumption of fossil fuels and allow that nonrenewable energy source to last longer.

Water (Hydro) Power

As with the wind, energy from the sun also causes the movement of water on Earth. This movement is called the *hydrologic cycle* (see Diagram 2). In the hydrologic cycle, water moves from the atmosphere by

51

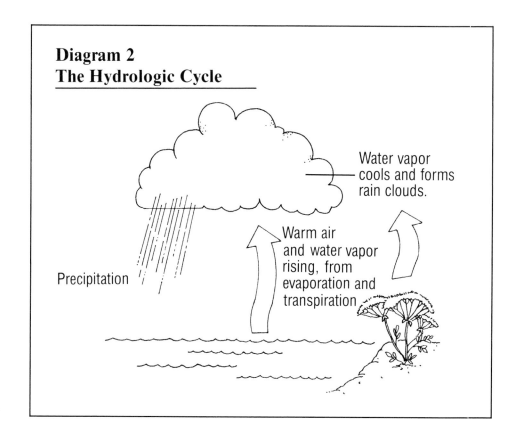

Diagram 2
The Hydrologic Cycle

Water vapor cools and forms rain clouds.

Warm air and water vapor rising, from evaporation and transpiration

Precipitation

precipitation (rain, snow, sleet, or hail), to the earth, and is returned to the atmosphere, as vapor, through *evaporation* and *transpiration,* in which water from living things becomes vapor. About one-third of the sun's energy is used to power the hydrologic cycle.

Much energy comes from moving water. Water falling is also a great source of energy. Waterfalls are used to turn water wheels, which, in turn, turn turbines, to produce electrical energy. Throughout the world, during the 1990s, one-fifth of the electrical power came from moving water.

Nuclear Energy

As was pointed out earlier, there are two types of nuclear energy, nuclear fission and nuclear fusion.

• *Nuclear fission.* Nuclear fission has been a practical energy source since the early 1960s. Today, many people look to this energy source as a solution to the problem of meeting most of the world's energy needs. The problem with nuclear fission, however, is the *radioactivity* of its fuel. Radioactive materials pose great dangers to life on Earth. Exposure to radioactive materials can cause cancer, mutations, sterility, and a host of other illnesses. The major danger in using radioactive materials lies in the chance of an accident, such as occurred in 1979 at Three Mile Island in the United States, and in 1986 at Chernobyl in the former Soviet Union. The other threat of nuclear fission to life on Earth comes from the disposal of nuclear wastes. Nuclear wastes remain radioactive for many, many years, so that safe disposal is limited at best. Many nuclear wastes have been buried in thick lead containers. These containers have been designed to last a long time, but how long? According to the United States Nuclear Regulatory Commission (NRC), it takes three million years for nuclear fuel wastes to return to their original levels of safe radioactivity. During this time it seems probable that some natural occurrence, such as an earthquake, might damage the containers.

If the United States built no more nuclear power plants than it had in 1992, it would still produce approximately 38,000 tons of nuclear waste annually.

• *Nuclear fusion.* Nuclear fusion, a process still in the early stages of development, could provide clean, safe, and efficient energy for the world. Fusion refers to the combining of atomic nuclei. When the nuclei of atoms are fused, enormous amounts of energy are released.

The fuels for fusion are *tritium* and *deuterium*. Tritium, which can be manufactured from naturally occurring lithium, is radioactive, but half disintegrates to a safe level within twelve years. Deuterium occurs naturally in every third water molecule. These fuels are relatively limitless and will provide a relatively harmless form of energy. Because the time it takes tritium to disintegrate to a safe level—a span of time known as *half-life*—is only twelve years, it makes nuclear fusion a relatively safe alternative to nuclear fission. Scientists project that the only waste product from fusion will be safe and clean helium gas.

Fusion reactors could convert energy to electricity. This would decrease our dependence upon fossil fuels and, eventually, replace them altogether. But fusion, as a practical form of energy, is still far in the future. The major problem is how to keep the fusion reaction going. It requires extremely high temperatures, like those on the sun, to get the nuclei of the deuterium atoms to fuse.

Project #10—
Nuclear Fission Energy

Background. There are enormous quantities of energy released by a small amount of nuclear fuel.

Materials Needed

a piece of chalk 15 mm (0.6 in) long	drawing paper
masking tape	pencil
	meterstick

Observations. Your observations will come from what you have read about nuclear energy and what you see happening during the experiment.

Hypothesis. If nuclear fuel produces more energy than fossil fuels, then it will take much less of it to produce an equal amount of energy.

Procedure.
1. Review the information in this book and from other sources on forms of energy. This will help you to get a perspective for the comparison you are about to make.

2. Measure a piece of chalk to 15 millimeters (0.6 inch) in length, and break it at that length. This piece represents one pellet of uranium, the fuel for nuclear fission.
3. Go to the corner of a room. The two walls of this corner will form two of the sides of a cube you will make with masking tape. Measure the corner to the following dimensions: 56 centimeters (22 inches) on the floor and walls. Use masking tape to mark off the area. You should have a cube 56 centimeters on each side (see Figure 16).

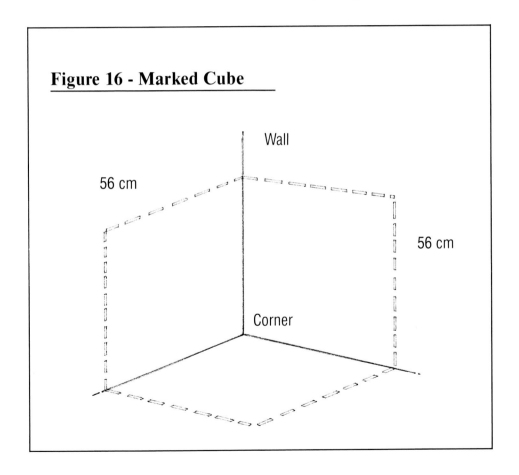

Figure 16 - Marked Cube

Wall

56 cm

56 cm

Corner

4. Place the chalk pellet (representing the uranium) in the square. This is enough uranium to equal the amount of energy produced if this entire cube were filled with oil.
5. Draw another cube 60 centimeters (24 inches) in this corner. This cube is drawn in the same manner as described above.
6. Place the chalk pellet inside this cube. This is enough uranium to equal the amount of energy produced if this entire cube were filled with hard-packed coal.

Record the results of the above two steps in your results.

Results.
1. What did you learn from the 56-cm cube?
2. What did you learn from the 60-cm cube?
3. How did your drawings show what you learned in this project?

Conclusion.   Was your hypothesis correct? Why or why not?

6

What Can You Do?

In the previous chapter, we explored clean, safe, and plentiful alternative forms of energy. None of these, however, has been developed to the point where it can replace fossil fuels as a major source of energy. What can we do here and now to offset our growing energy crisis—without harming our environment?

CONSERVING THROUGH EFFICIENCY

One obvious answer is to conserve fossil fuel energy through efficiency. During the early 1990s, studies showed that the United States wasted one-half of the energy it consumed. Heat escaping from poorly insulated homes and excess burning of gasoline and oil in cars, due to poor maintenance, are just two examples of wasted fossil fuel energy. Below are some areas in which you can save energy and conserve fossil fuels.

In Your Home
• Make sure your home is properly insulated. If every home in the United States were insulated properly, Americans could save enough natural gas to heat over four million homes.
• Lower the winter temperature in your home and raise the summer temperature. If every house in the United States lowered its average win-

Recycling newspapers helps to save not only trees, which provide the raw material for paper, but also the energy required to manufacture, transport, and dispose of paper.

ter temperature six degrees over a 24-hour period, Americans would save approximately 570,000 barrels of heating oil per day. If we raised the temperature six degrees in the summer, we would save 190,000 barrels of oil used to run air conditioners per day.

• Energy-efficient appliances can also save a great deal of energy. Energy can also be saved by not running appliances unless absolutely necessary, and by keeping the appliances in good working order.

Project #11—Insulation

Background.   The background for this experiment comes from what you have read on insulation.

Materials Needed

Pyrex beaker	water
Styrofoam insulated cup	scissors
Celsius thermometer	compass
cardboard	ruler
	paper and pencil

Observations.   Your observations will come from what you have read about insulation and from your experience investigating insulation.

Inference.   Insulation protects against heat loss.

Hypothesis.   If insulation protects against heat loss, then an insulated container will retain heat longer than an uninsulated container.

Procedure.
1. Cut out two cardboard lids, one for the Pyrex beaker and one for the Styrofoam cup. Do this by measuring the inside diameter of the cup rim and then, using a compass, make a circle on the cardboard. Cut the circle out with a scissors.

2. Place equal amounts of hot water in the Pyrex beaker and Styrofoam cup. Measure the temperature of the water in each container. Record it in Results.
3. Place the cardboard lids on the cups, and let the cups stand for one minute. Record the temperature. Record the temperature each minute for five more minutes.

Results.
Temperature

At Start	1 min.	2 min.	3 min.	4 min.	5 min.
Beaker					
Styrofoam cup					

Conclusion. Was your hypothesis correct or incorrect? Why or why not? Which material—glass or Styrofoam—is the better insulator?

Recycling

Recycling also saves energy and conserves our natural resources. A ton of oil is saved when a ton of iron ore is recycled. Recycling paper saves approximately 25 to 70 percent of the energy used in its manufacture from virgin materials. Such energy savings make recycling worthwhile.

An additional advantage to recycling is that it cuts down on the amount of solid waste in the environment. In the early 1990s, the Environmental Protection Agency estimated that by the year 2000 more than half the states in the United States will run out of places to put garbage. This garbage overflow will require increased use of incinerators, which, in turn, pollute the atmosphere.

7

The Future

With every passing year, our fossil fuel energy resources dwindle. Still, we burn vast amounts of these fuels in order to maintain our quality of life. But how much longer can we continue on this course?

The United States and the other industrialized nations need to adopt national energy policies that provide for safe and efficient choices. By doing this, they could alleviate global tensions, improve the quality of the environment, and conserve our fossil fuel supplies.

Government leaders must enact strict energy laws and national energy strategies that will ensure the future of the world. They could do this by providing tax breaks and other incentives for alternative energy research, development, and use.

At the First Annual United Nations Conference on Environment and Development, in 1992, it was made clear that we must make a commitment to reduce our dependence on fossil fuels. The world must develop energy technologies that use safe, renewable sources of fuel. Nations and individuals must make an effort to conserve energy.

We must act now, as a global community, together. We have reached the stage in human development where we are no longer a group of individual nations. We are a global ecosystem, with all the nations of the world connected to and dependent upon one another. What is good for one is good for all, and the converse. The future belongs to us. Let's move to make it safe and secure for all humanity and other living things.

Conclusions to Projects

Project 1. My hypothesis was correct because light energy was transferred and transformed into heat. The black box and can absorbed and converted more light energy into heat.

Project 2. My hypothesis was correct because, in the transfer of heat energy from the water to the washers, there was a heat loss. I saw this by measuring the loss with a calorimeter.

Project 3. My hypothesis was correct because only the plant that received light, water, and carbon dioxide gas survived. The other plants died.

Project 4. My hypothesis was correct because the aquatic food chain did successfully transfer energy. Herbivores got energy from producers, carnivores from herbivores, omnivores from both herbivores and carnivores.

Project 5. My hypothesis was correct because the plant was harmed. The coleus plant exposed to SO_2 gas lost color and became very unhealthy.

Project 6. My hypothesis was correct because the oil spill prevented the plants from carrying on the process of photosynthesis. As the oil covered the surface, it blocked the necessary light energy.

Project 7. My hypothesis was correct because the incomplete combustion of fossil fuels does put harmful particulates into the environment. The soot and particles on the card can get into people's lungs and cause harm.

Project 8. My hypothesis was correct because solar energy did cook the hot dog. The radiant energy from the sun, when focused on the meat, cooked it until it sizzled and the skin split.

Project 9. My hypothesis was correct because the wind direction was from west to east most of the time. Therefore, the wind did blow counterclockwise.

My hypothesis was incorrect because the wind direction was not from west to east because (variable) _____ .

Project 10. My hypothesis was correct because it takes much less nuclear fuel than fossil fuel to produce an equal amount of energy. The fuel space required for fossil fuels was much greater than the space required for nuclear fuels.

Project 11. My hypothesis was correct because the water in the insulated Styrofoam cup stayed warmer. I saw this when I measured the temperature of the water in each cup.

Glossary

Acid Rain. Rainwater containing acids that have formed from the combination of sulfur dioxide, nitric oxide, or nitrogen dioxide gases with water vapor.

Adenosine Triphosphate (ATP). A chemical made in green plants from light energy. It is used to split the water molecule into its component parts of two hydrogen atoms and one oxygen atom.

Big Bang Theory. A theory that our universe was created from a massive explosion of gases and particles.

Biomass. Nonliving or waste material that can be used to produce energy.

Biosphere. Any place on Earth that will support life.

Calorimeter. A device that measures the amount of heat that will raise the temperature of one gram of water one degree Celsius.

Carbon Dioxide Gas (CO_2). A colorless, odorless, tasteless gas found naturally in small amounts in the air.

Carnivore. Any animal that only eats flesh.

Chlorophyll. A green-colored chemical found in plants. It is the only substance on Earth that can take light energy and convert it into chemical energy. This energy is used to manufacture food.

Chloroplast. A small, disc-like cell, found in green plants, which contains chlorophyll.

Classification. Arranging objects or events in some order according to their properties.

Conclusion. A statement after a scientific experiment stating whether a hypothesis was correct or incorrect and why.

Consumer. Any animal in the food chain that eats green plants or flesh for energy.

Detritus Food Chain. The food chain of the decomposers, which break down dead and waste material and return it to the soil in the form of nutrients.

Deuterium. A fuel for nuclear fusion. It is found in every third water molecule.

Dissolved Oxygen. Oxygen found in water and used by aquatic life forms in respiration.

Ecology. The study of how all living things interrelate with each other and their nonliving environment.

Energy. The ability to do work.

Evaporation. Water rising into the air as a gas.

First Law of Motion. A body at rest will stay at rest until an outside force puts it into motion, and a body in motion will remain in motion until an outside force stops it.

First Law of Thermodynamics. Energy cannot be created or destroyed, but can be transferred and transformed.

Force. A push or pull on an object.

Fossil Fuel. Any fuel formed from the fossil remains of plants or animals, such as coal, oil, or natural gas.

Geothermal Energy. Energy produced by heat inside the earth.

Glucose. A simple sugar ($C_6H_{12}O_6$) produced by green plants in the process of photosynthesis.

Grazing Food Chain. The system of relationships between living things that depend upon one another for energy in the form of food.

Greenhouse Effect. A process by which certain gases (such as carbon dioxide, water vapor, methane, sulfur dioxide) trap the sun's heat close to the earth's surface, consequently causing global warming.

Half-Life. The time required for half of the atoms of a radioactive substance to disintegrate.

Herbivore. Any animal that eats only green plants.

Hydrologic Cycle. The regular movement of water from the atmosphere, by precipitation, to the earth's surface, and its return to the atmosphere by evaporation and transpiration.

Hypothesis. An inference or prediction that can be tested; usually stated as an if-then sentence.

Incomplete Combustion. The condition that results when a fuel is not burned completely due to lack of oxygen.

Inertia. A principle included in Newton's first law of motion, and referring to the tendency of a moving object to remain moving until an outside force stops it.

Inference. An educated guess, based on what you have observed about something that has happened.

Internal-Combustion Engine. An engine in which the fuel is burned within the engine itself, rather than in an external furnace.

Kinetic Energy. The energy of motion.

Natural Gas. A fossil fuel coming from the earth's crust, through natural openings or bored wells. Often found with or near petroleum.

Nonrenewable Natural Resource. Any natural resource that is available only in limited quantities; includes substances that take so many years to develop that they are considered nonreplaceable, such as fossil fuels.

Nuclear Fission. An atomic reaction in which the nucleus of the atom is split, creating vast amounts of heat and light.

Nuclear Fusion. An atomic reaction in which the nuclei of atoms are fused, creating vast amounts of heat and light.

Nutrient. A nourishing substance necessary for the growth and health of living things.

Observation. The first step in the scientific method; it involves using all your senses to find out all you can about an object. Observations can also be made through research.

Omnivore. Any animal that eats both flesh and vegetation.

Organism. Any living thing.

Oxygen (O_2). A gas that makes up 21 percent of the air. Required by most living things in order to exist.

Ozone (O_3). An active form of oxygen. In the stratosphere, it forms the protective layer that blocks the sun's harmful rays.

Particulate. A particle, in the air, such as soot.

Peat. The first material that develops in the formation of coal.

Petroleum. A carbon-based liquid fossil fuel found in the crust of the earth.

Photosynthesis. A process by which green plants make food (the simple sugar glucose) and give off oxygen.

Photovoltaic Energy. A form of energy that converts light energy directly into electrical energy, through a photovoltaic cell, which is made of thin layers of semiconductor material.

Potential Energy. Stored energy.

Precipitation. Water falling from the atmosphere in such forms as rain, snow, sleet, and hail.

Predator. Any animal that hunts and captures its prey.

Prediction. An educated guess, based upon what you have observed, about something that is going to happen.

Pressure Gradient Force. The flow of wind, from high pressure to low pressure.

Producer. Any organism that manufactures its own food; specifically, green plants.

Property. In classification by the scientific method, something that belongs to an object, which helps to identify the object.

Radioactivity. The process by which atoms emit high-energy particles and rays, by disintegration of their nuclei.

Recycling. A method of reprocessing and reusing products.

Results. A step in the scientific method that involves determining what happened in an experiment.

Second Law of Motion. A small force will move an object slowly. A large force will move it rapidly. An object always moves in the same direction as a force.

Second Law of Thermodynamics. When energy is transferred or transformed, some of it enters a state in which it becomes useless.

Soda Lime Crystals. A carbon dioxide absorbent.

Solar Energy. Energy from the sun.

Solar-Thermal Energy System. An energy system in which the sun's rays are used to heat liquids.

Sulfur Dioxide Gas (SO_2). A compound formed both naturally and by the combustion of coal or oil, both of which contain sulfur. When combined with water vapor, sulfur dioxide forms sulfuric acid, an ingredient of acid rain.

Third Law of Motion. For every action there is an equal and opposite reaction along the same straight line.

Transpiration. Water released into the air by plants, through their stoma (pores).

Tritium. A radioactive fuel, manufactured from naturally occurring lithium, which has a half-life of only twelve years, used in nuclear fusion.

Variable. Uncontrolled conditions that can affect the outcome of a scientific investigation (for example, air temperature, moisture, or the like).

Work. The exertion of force, on an object, over a distance.

Further Reading

Corson, Walter H. *The Global Ecology Handbook*. New York: Global Tomorrow Coalition, 1990.

Cross, Wilbur. *Petroleum*. Chicago: Childrens Press, 1983.

Earth Works Group. *50 Simple Things You Can Do to Save the Earth*. Kansas City, MO: Earthworks Press, 1990.

Gutnik, Martin J. *How to Do a Science Project and Report*. New York: Franklin Watts, 1980.

Gutnik, Martin J. *The Challenge of Clean Air*. Hillside, NJ: Enslow Publishers, Inc., 1990.

Kraft, Betsy H. *Oil and Natural Gas*. Revised edition. New York: Franklin Watts, 1982.

Lee, Sally. *The Throwaway Society*. New York: Franklin Watts, 1990.

Wood, Geraldine and Harold. *Pollution*. New York: Franklin Watts, 1985.

Index